MAGNIFICENT HORSES OF THE WORLD

LIPIZZANER HORSES

For a free color catalog describing Gareth Stevens' list of high-quality books, call 1-800-542-2595 (USA) or 1-800-461-9120 (Canada). Gareth Stevens' Fax: (414) 225-0377.

Library of Congress Cataloging-in-Publication Data available upon request from publisher.
Fax: (414) 225-0377 for the attention of the Publishing Records Department.

ISBN 0-8368-1371-5

This edition first published in North America in 1995 by
Gareth Stevens Publishing
1555 North RiverCenter Drive, Suite 201
Milwaukee, Wisconsin 53212, USA

First published in Great Britain in 1994 by Sunburst Books, Deacon House, 65 Old Church Street, London, SW3 5BS.
Photographs © 1989 Franckh'sche Verlagshandlung, W. Keller & Co., Stuttgart, Germany. Text © 1994 Sunburst Books.
Additional end matter © 1995 by Gareth Stevens, Inc.

U.S. Series Editor: Patricia Lantier-Sampon
U.S. Editor: Barbara J. Behm

Printed in Mexico.

2 3 4 5 6 7 8 9 9 99 98 97 96

MAGNIFICENT HORSES OF THE WORLD

LIPIZZANER HORSES

Photography by
Tomáš Míček
Elisabeth Kellner

Text by
Dr. Hans-Jörg Schrenk

Gareth Stevens Publishing
MILWAUKEE

The Lipizzaner (also spelled Lippizaner) is a world-famous show horse. Lipizzaners are known for their strength, elegance, and ability to perform complex movements.

Lipizzaners are bred and trained mainly in Vienna, Austria, at an establishment called the Spanish Riding School.

Lipizzaners are small, compact horses with long backs, thick necks, and muscular legs.

The mares and foals spend all day in the meadows and are brought back to the stables only when temperatures become very hot.

Every horse lover who has seen them is captivated by the Lipizzaners of the Spanish Riding School. Watching the Lipizzaner stallions perform with their riders dressed in brown tails is an unforgettable experience. The Lipizzaners are one of the oldest breeds of horse in the world. They have been bred specifically for the Spanish Riding School for over four hundred years. The school was founded in 1572 to instruct noblemen in classical horseback riding.

The Lipizzaner, a descendant of the Spanish Andalusian horse, carries itself with great presence.

A Lipizzaner releases pent-up energy with a series of wild leaps and gallops.

Outside of Vienna, Lipizzaners are also bred in many of the countries that used to be part of the former Austro-Hungarian Empire. Although the Lipizzaners originated from the Andalusian line, other ancestors include the Arabian, Neapolitan, and Kladruber horses.

This foal is just a few days old and still has its grayish-brown coat. The final color of the Lipizzaner's coat can only be determined when the horse is fully mature between the ages of five and seven years.

A mare and her foal. The first white hairs have appeared on the foal.

Foals always return to their mothers to nurse, no matter how plentiful the pasture is.

During the Baroque era (the seventeenth and first half of the eighteenth centuries), Spanish horses were considered to be the best thoroughbred riding and carriage horses. Ownership of these horses was a status symbol in all the royal courts of Europe. The Spanish horses, also known as Andalusians, were a cross between the heavy, native horses of Spain and the horses belonging to the Berbers of Arabia. The Berbers came to Spain in the eighth century, when Spain was conquered by the Moors. When it eventually became too expensive to import horses for the royal stables directly from Spain, many European courts began to establish their own breeding areas.

The magnificent Lipizzaner stallions were originally bred for use in battle. Soldiers on the backs of the Lipizzaners maneuvered their stallions to perform incredible leaps and plunges that frightened the enemy foot soldiers into retreating. During modern times, Lipizzaner stallions still perform these spectacular leaps.
But this time, the result is applause and admiration from horse lovers around the world.

Lipizzaners are known as "ballet dancers of the world" because of their incredible agility.

*Lipizzaners at
full gallop.*

The breed originated in 1580 in the small town of Lipica (also known as Lipizza) near the city of Trieste, in Italy (once part of the Austrian empire). In that year, 9 stallions and 24 mares were imported from the Iberian Peninsula at the order of Archduke Charles II of Austria. These horses were the initial stock for breeding parade-horses for the imperial court in Vienna. The royal family of Austria, the Hapsburgs, were the owners of the horses. No common person was allowed to own a Lipizzaner. However, nobles serving with the Hapsburg armies were given Lipizzaners to ride. The Spanish Andalusians were crossed with the strong, stocky, native Italian horses, whose endurance and strength had been praised since Roman times. Another ancestor of the Lipizzaner was the Neapolitan, a cross between Andalusian and Arabian horses that was popular during the Baroque era because of its slow, high-stepping gait (the Spanish gait).

Since the eighteenth century, the Lipizzaner has been bred from six classic lines.

The horses at Lipica often had to be evacuated to protect them from attack during times of war. In 1797, the herd was rescued from the approaching French army and set out on a forty-day march to Hungary. After six months, the horses were returned to Lipica. In 1805, they had to leave their home once again. Through ice and snow, the horses were moved to Slovenia, where they stayed for two years before their return in 1807. In 1809, they had to be evacuated again, this time to Hungary, where they remained until 1815.

World War II almost put an end to the Lipizzaners. Many of the horses were rounded up and held by the German army. It was only thanks to the combined efforts of the director of the Spanish Riding School, their breeding manager, and United States Army General George Patton that the herd of about three hundred survived the threat of the approaching Russian front. The story of this incident is told in the Walt Disney movie, *Miracle of the White Stallions.*

It was in the early nineteenth century that, because of an increased number of thoroughbred Arabians being used for breeding, gray became the hallmark color of the Lipizzaner.

Although the Lipizzaner is not built to be a fast horse, its powerful hindquarters do enable it to perform complex show movements. The "dancing Lipizzaners" of the famous Knie Circus are known and admired throughout the world. The precise, perfect movements of these horses are possible only after years of rigorous training.

For the first few months, young stallions are trained on a lunging rein. In this early time, the young horses learn to obey commands and to trust their trainers. Next, the young stallions are ridden. At first, they simply learn to go forward. But mainly they are learning to understand and follow the riders' directions. Then they can learn the walk, trot, and canter. Over time, the lessons become more and more complex. After a great deal of training, the horses become more flexible, and they are better able to balance themselves. The end result is graceful movement and absolute control of their muscles to make a stunning and seemingly effortless performance.

A feature that Lipizzaners inherited from Arabian horses was their distinctive nose.

The Lipizzaner is one of the most athletic and intelligent of all the horse breeds. It has short, powerful limbs with flat joints and strong bones. Lipizzaners stand 59-62 inches (150-157 centimeters) tall. They weigh an imposing 1,000-1,300 pounds (450-585 kilograms). They have hard hooves as a result of the rocky, limestone country surrounding Lipica. Lipizzaners have a calm, placid temperament, making them very disciplined students.

Lipizzaners are probably the rarest, most aristocratic breed of horse in the world. They are descended from six lines of stallions named Pluto, Conversano, Neapolitano, Favory, Maestoso, and Siglavy, and eighteen families of mares.

Foals are born black or brown in color, but as they grow, they can turn a pure white.

A mare is caught off-guard by the camera.

The heads of Lipizzaners are beautifully shaped as influenced by the Arabians and Andalusians.

Besides the classically trained Lipizzaners, there are other types, as well. Some Lipizzaners are bred mainly as workhorses. These horses are ideally suited for agricultural work because they are heavier and smaller than the school horses. A bigger, free-moving Lipizzaner, perfect for pulling carriages, is bred in Hungary. The Lipizzaner is also appreciated as an outstanding recreational riding horse. The powerful haunches, strong backs, intelligence, and grace of all the Lipizzaners have made this a popular horse the world over.

A young stallion in profile.

Lipizzaners, as show horses, possess the grace and strength to perform highly intricate movements.

The days of the Lipizzaner as the parade horse of the royal courts were over long ago. Today, these horses are ideal for leisure riding. Good-natured and intelligent, they are a versatile recreational and sport horse. They are particularly successful in driving competitions. In Hungary, Lipizzaners are crossed with trotters to improve their chances of winning international horse races.

At full gallop. Tails of the Lipizzaners are silky and set high.

Two young stallions. Stallions and mares are put through performance tests before they are allowed to breed.

This Lipizzaner demonstrates the powerful elegance of this ancient breed.

Lipizzaner mares move slowly across the wide expanses of pasture at evening sun.

A Lipizzaner mare enjoys a summer day. The breeding lines of the distinguished Lipizzaners began to be recorded in 1735.

A herd of mares grazes at Lipica.

This magnificent stallion has earned a fine reputation at the Spanish Riding School.

*Lipizzaners at the Spanish Riding School enjoy rolling in the snow
after their day is done.*

The dark and watchful eye of a world-famous Lipizzaner.

GLOSSARY

ancestors — the living things from which another living thing is descended.

breed — animals having specific traits; to produce offspring.

canter — a slow, easy gallop.

compact — tightly packed together.

evacuate — to leave a dangerous place.

foals — newborn male or female horses.

gait — a way of walking or running.

gallop — a fast way of running by an animal, such as a horse.

graze — to feed on grass or other plants.

haunches — the hip, buttocks, and upper thigh.

herd — a number of animals of one kind that stay together and travel as a group.

lunging rein — a long, narrow strap used by a rider or driver to control an animal.

mares — female horses.

stallions — mature male horses used for breeding.

thoroughbred — a horse or another animal that is bred from the best blood through a long line.

trot — a four-legged animal's slow running gait.

MORE BOOKS ABOUT HORSES

Album of Horses. Marguerite Henry (Macmillan)
Complete Book of Horses and Horsemanship. C. W. Anderson (Macmillan)
The Great Book of Horses. Catherine Dell (R. Rourke)
Guide to the Horses of the World. Caroline Silver (Exeter)
Horse Breeds and Breeding. Jane Kidd (Crescent)
Horse Happy: A Complete Guide to Owning Your Own Horse. Barbara J. Berry (Bobbs-Merrill)
Horses and Riding. George Henschel (Franklin Watts)
The Ultimate Horse Book. Elwyn Hartley Edwards (Dorling Kindersley)
Wild and Wonderful Horses. Cristopher Brown, ed. (Antioch)
Yesterday's Horses. Jean S. Doty (Macmillan)

VIDEOS

The Art of Riding Series. (Visual Education Productions)
The Horse Family. (International Film Bureau)
Horses! (Encyclopedia Britannica)
The Mare and Foal. (Discovery Trail)
Nature: Wild Horses. (Warner Home Video)

Places to Write

Here are some places to write for more information about horses. When you write, include your name and address, and be specific about the information you would like to receive. Don't forget to enclose a stamped, self-addressed envelope for a reply.

National Association for Humane
   and Environmental Education
P.O. Box 362
East Haddam, CT 06423-0362

Horse Council of British Columbia
5746B 176A Street
Cloverdale, British Columbia
V3S 4C7

Index